Visual Field

Jan Haag

BookLeaf
Publishing

India | USA | UK

Made with ❤ on the BookLeaf Publishing Platform

www.bookleafpub.in

www.bookleafpub.com

Dedication

To those who shaped me into a poet—so many poets and teachers I can't begin to count or name them all.

For my mother who likes everything I write, and my sisters (by birth and by choice) who helped grow me into a writer.

And for Georgann, who claimed me as her BFF and never let go—even in death, thank goodness.

And for Clifford, who had to go, and Dickie, who came back, forever cheering me on.

Preface

I climb a flight of stairs to the second floor of the health care facility where a terrific optometrist has been taking care of my eyes for years. I figure the stairs are good for my heart. My optometrist is, naturally, much more interested in my eyes, especially now that she's treating me for early-stage glaucoma.

I'm here for my biannual visual field test, or, more formally, the automated static perimetry test. I sit in a darkened room looking into a bowl-shaped device, wearing a jaunty pirate's eyepatch, stare at a small yellow fixed light with my uncovered right eye and apply my index finger to a clicker when I see pinpoints of light quickly flash inside the bowl. A technician administers the test and tells me when to switch they patch to my other eye.

I used to hate these tests. I'd get hot and light-headed inside the machine, which always felt stuffy to me. Anxiety crawled up my neck like a spider, as I'd fear that this would be the time when my results were so bad that I'd have to start daily glaucoma drops. My mother has done this for years, and, at age 93, she is quickly losing her vision.

I could see my future in my now-tiny mother who reluctantly gave up driving a couple of years ago and gave her car to me. Now my sister and I are two of several drivers who chauffeur her where she needs to go. And she's a busy gal, on the move five days a week.

Watching one's peripheral field of vision decrease and the whole world darken is a scary prospect, to say the least. My mother is, as she has long been, a role model in this, showing me how it's done with grace and grit. Still, no one likes to think about or watch her vision dim until she is quite literally left in the dark.

But then there are the people I've known, some dear friends and some acquaintances, who have been blind all their lives. They've been excellent role models—men and woman with low vision who've not only adapted but thrived as professional and creative people. Their visual impairments are just one facet of their being—far from the whole story—and, using the tremendous technology available today, they demonstrate again and again that this condition is one I can learn to embrace, too.

 Today's visual field test went well, I think, though glaucoma is not a condition that typically improves with time. The hope is to slow down the progression of the disease. But I have an even greater appreciation for my sight and, in my mid-60s, am taking greater care of my eyes, widening my visual field psychically and spiritually, if not physically.

I apply daily drops to help control eye pressure. I take supplements to help boost my immune system and wear sunglasses outside. I wear glasses at the computer to help with eyestrain and step away from the screen more frequently than I used to.

And after a long career as a journalist, editor and college writing professor, I lead writing workshops in my happily retired life. And I write poetry, posting poems every day on social media and on my website (janishaag.com).

As a lifelong writer, I have written myself out of more difficulties than I can count, and chronicled endless surprises and joys, too. My creative visual field widens with each piece I write; my heart expands, too. I find myself awash in gratitude for my lucky, lovely life, as I've often said, and to those who have paved a path that I continue to follow, delighted at what my five senses encounter along the way.

Jan Haag
Sacramento, California

Pour me a cup of words

Thank you, and yes, a splash of simile
and two full teaspoons of metaphor,
stirred with fresh images

and not a little rhythm to bounce
the lines merrily along, so smoothly
that a reader finds herself

effortlessly pulled along with every
bit of nuance, not noticing the
subtle off-rhyme,

which, it turns out, you didn't intend
but there it landed, one of those
serendipitous bits of

literary sweetness that fills the cup,
all those letters floating on the surface,
just waiting to be sipped

into something, like this, that looks
like a poem.

Acknowledgements

"This longest night" was published by Birdland Journal, spring 2020 issue

"Stopped" and "You don't notice the dying leaving" were published on Salt Water (findyourharbor.com)

Other poems can be found on janishaag.com.

1. Visual field

Put your chin in the little dip
and look into the bowl of stars,
tiny suns that blink and disappear,

then press with an eager finger
the button to indicate that some
part of your peripheral vision

has noted them. But immediately
you wonder, *Did I really see that?*
Was it an eyeblink or a floater?

Because you fear that you cannot
trust what you think you see, no matter
how tack sharp or dull your sight.

It is the sense you most rely on,
you and you and me, too, so you
sigh during this test, try to relax

your shoulders, breathe as normally
as you can, soften your focus and
imagine looking through a telescope

at a thousand, ten thousand suns
winking at you from a great distance,
casting light thousands of years old,

and you, lucky one, catch glints
as quick as a whisper into the cosmic
past, your eyes not deceiving you,

letting the light in, as they are meant to,
you wide-eyed, wonderful thing,
you.

2. Beginner

Be willing to be a beginner every single morning.
— Meister Eckhart

My favorite students to teach, those summer
mornings at the high school pool, were
the Beginners. A couple levels up from

Non-Swimmers, still tentative, some reluctant
to put their faces in the water. They taught me
that insisting they do it my way did not work,

that for some, just blowing bubbles on
the crystalline blue surface was a brave act,
or trusting the water to hold them when

they stretched out on their backs, little chests
puffed up toward the sun, my hand barely
between their shoulder blades for reassurance.

I'd whisper in their ears, half above the surface,
You're floating! and they'd grin and start to giggle,
flailing and sputtering as I caught them.

Try again, I'd say. *Take a deep breath. I've got you.*

And now I wonder where such insight bubbled
up in a 16-year-old girl, herself a beginner,

barely launched in life, in love. Or was I giving
myself advice I'd later need for the journey,
for the beginnings that would inevitably arrive

unbidden, requiring a starting over, a call to
embark again, always the neophyte, the perpetual
apprentice with so much to learn?

3. Three sisters

(for Sue and Donna)

Two of us were born to my mother,
the other, next door best friend, to another mother,
who is now gone, but who was part of the village

that raised us all, we three aware of time
not so much passing as disappearing on a poof
of cloud scudding across hazy summer sky.

I cannot imagine my childhood without either of them,
me bookended by the tall one eight months older
and the blonde one younger by two years

and three months—each of those months counting
hugely when we were girls to advance us further
into the world, farther from the lakeside circle

where we grew. As neighbors, as Scouts, as band
mates, as carpool buddies—our mothers in bridge
foursomes, who drove the carpools and schlepped

kids miles into town, who fed us and kept us
clothed and nudged us to practice our instruments

and came to every band concert Who made us

believe that we could do anything, be anything
we wanted. And we did. We are, each of us
60-somethings, so far from our 8- and 6-year-old

selves who met when one set of parents set
us down next door to the other, and three girls
met, one of them a solo act, probably never

dreaming she'd end up part of a trio, just as
the duet never imagined a third. But here
we are, my dears. Here we so blessedly are.

4. Mother's lilacs

She wanted to walk down the hill
of backyard lawn to see the lilac
in full bloom up close—prime
time for her favorite plant
at its fragrant peak.

So, as I watered the potted plants
on the patio, she carefully made
her way to the lawn, urging me to
come with her. Now that she finds
it difficult to detect nuances in
bright light and deep shadow,
I'm inclined to follow.

So I set down the hose, trailing
my mother to the slender tree
set into the ground years earlier,
after another longtime resident
had died.

It's supposed to be a bush,
Mother said, *but it's tall—*
not a solid profusion of flowers
but one oblong globe per branch.

She stood a respectful distance
away while I zeroed in on a
particular blossom for a sniff
and a sigh.

Still, she was not close enough
to inhale that heady fragrance
she loves, so fleeting it'll disappear
in a couple of weeks or so.

Let's go see the other one,
she said, already heading
off across the grass.

Though she couldn't see it from
where we stood, she knew that
the other lilac had twined itself
amid the towering oleanders, and,
when she reached the shade line,
she stopped.

Can you see them? she asked.
Yes, I said. *Right in front of you.
Overhead, too. It's dripping with lilacs.*

Still she stayed rooted,
and put her slender, ringed

fingers into my hand so I could
lead her slowly into shadow.

Oh, now I see it, she said, freeing
her fingers to touch and linger
on the tight clusters.

Here's one low enough to smell, I said,
but she didn't move till I took her hand
again and guided her to the nose-high
blossom. She inhaled, smiling into lilac
memories rising with the molecules
of a scent she has long loved.

Oh, yes, she said.
Oh, yes.

And we stood in the shade together
a bit longer before moving, each of us,
back into the light.

5. Swim

*"...we are always fish in the belly of the whale of earth.
We are encased and can't stray from the house of our
bodies."*
    —from "Spring," Jim Harrison

•••

(for Kristie McCleary)

But what if you could find your way
out of the whale's belly,
kick through humble earth
and emerge, your grit-caked,
fishy self, finning through air?

What if, set free in another form,
you don't need to see or even breathe?
Unbound, you surf currents of wind,
swim toward whatever catches
your fancy, the flicker on the edge—

the jasmine blooming on the fence,
the smudge of fat-blossomed rose,

a loved one's face you know by touch.

Aim for the moon,
you, the untethered, the unblooded.
There is no need to become;
you have arrived.
You are there.

6. We two, dreaming

(for Georgann)

Do you dream me now
as I do you?
Are we together in your
place of mystery?

Please let us sit side by side
your head on my shoulder
or minc on yours.

Let us both be embodied,
arms touching, shadowed
in dreams, surrounded
by the wagging tongues
of anthuriums set into a bed
of stars. No need to speak.

My hand on you,
your hand on me,
dreaming our separate
dreams together
forever and ever
amene.

7. Quiet, please

Listen,
the voice said,
and I did,
sit,
and I did,
resisting the urge
to ask why,
and the voice
said, *rest a bit,*
honey, your soul
wants to catch up,

and I thought,
you mean I can
outrun my soul?
isn't it like a shadow,
always attached?

and the voice
sighed,
as it does,
and said,
shhhh, honey,
lie down,

close your eyes,

and if the
voice had
had a finger, it
would've put
it on my lips
before I could
say,

but I thought
I *had* slowed
down, this
is not my
old speed,
and how
will I know
when my soul
has caught up?
will it tap me
on the shoulder,
saying, we can
go now?

and the voice
shhhhhh'd me,
melting my

eyelids,
whispering,
rest now,
honey.
give it
a little time.
you'll know.

8. Eyedrops

(for Marie Reynolds)

Two minutes, lying down,
index fingers pressing the corners
of each eye after you maneuver
a single drop in.

You add the lying down part
to the prescription, along with
the timer on the iPad and its
serene bell, the same one that
once reverbcrated around your
late poet friend's living room,
she a slight and graceful presence
with a bunch of poets reviewing
their drafty drafts, 10 minutes
apiece, the gentle sound signaling
time to move on!

And each time you hear it now,
the twice-a-day tintinnabulation,
lying on your bed, finger pressure
preventing the drops from sliding
down your nasal passages, you

wonder if she heard such a chime
near her end, nudging her on.

Today, though it is noon,
you hear the *hooooo, hoo-hoo*
of mourning dove (which for years
you spelled *morning*) outside your
window, and you smile, eyes
closed, stinging a bit as they do,

and when the chime bongs its
soft bong, you lie there for a bit,
listening to it diminish, knowing
that it will not sound again
until it's completely drifted
away.

So you wait for it,
like the dove, like her smile,
to circle round again,
not wanting in the least
to move on.

9. Into the darkness you go

Like the ride that takes you into the tunnel,
soundless but for water displaced by your small boat,
breath, heartbeat, and if you are lucky,

there's a hand close by that might take yours,
a reassuring palm press, a reminder
that this is not just a time to be endured

but savored, that the darkness—*hello, old friend—*
holds you differently but holds you nonetheless
you and your tiny boat, floating, moving

slowly toward the inevitable light.

10. Mansuetude

(for Clifford)

noun [man-swi-tood, -tyood]: mildness; gentleness

Is it because he was a man
that I found this his most
attractive quality—

his mildness, his gentleness,
his great heart, which,
by the time it stopped,

had grown three times
its normal size thanks to
malformed valves?

What if those leaky
flaps that never fully
closed and jacked up

his heart muscle like
an iron-pumping
bodybuilder

were what made him
such a gentle man
with such capacity

for love, the kind
that echoes around me
to this day, that

somehow powers
the beat of my own
imperfect heart?

11. Shadow walk

for my mother

Our shadows walk side by side,
yours pushing the apparatus that

helps you stand taller, ache less,
and in our shadows I imagine

a much younger you pushing
a much younger me

in a different kind of rolling
contraption, perhaps just as

slowly, with great deliberation,
moving the two of us then

from there to here. And
here we are now,

in a here we could not have
envisioned in the then.

But here we still are,

walking beside each other,

me and my shadow,
you and yours.

And this is what I promise
to remember in the someday

when my shadow walks
alone—our silhouettes,

just like this,
in the forever here.

12. Opened

You, who have been split open
by love or loss or both,
somehow still stand,
though you have no idea
why.

You wonder if this gash,
reopened far too many times,
can possibly heal—
perhaps with divine sutures—
so that one day you'll barely
perceive the trace of a scar.

It seems impossible
to your hollowed-out self,
but, dear one, trust us—

healing happens in the shadows
where there is always a little light,
even if your weary eyes can't
perceive it.

What has enriched you—
and, yes, opened you

in joy and grief —
can one day fill you
again.

In fact, it already has.

13. Stopped

(for Dickie)

Before my brain could begin
to process it—you, falling to the airport
floor, pulse fluttering in your neck
until someone rolled you onto your back,
and the fluttering stopped—
Loss opened the shuttered door
in my heart, walked through again,
stood next to me, put his arm
around me, said, *There, there.*

We stood there, Loss and I,
watching as strangers knelt around
you, a perfect halo of helpers.
Grief showed up, lending his warmth
to our little huddle. *Hey, girl,*
said Grief, old friend that he is.
Don't watch—or maybe, do.
It'll help later.

Then Hope joined us, nudging me.
Take a picture, honey, she whispered.
If he comes back, he'll ask

if you got a picture.

That made me smile; Hope knows
us so well. I extracted myself
from Grief's gentle arms and said,
Excuse me, without explanation,
because Grief understands.

I stepped into the glory of humanity
around you, took out my phone and
snapped an image of you there,
a large man compressing your chest,
a smaller one holding your head,
checking your pulse, another arriving
with a machine, someone placing
pads with wires on your ribs.

You know," Loss whispered, trying
to prepare me, *this doesn't always
work.*

But Hope grabbed my hand and,
though no one else did, sang out,
Clear! a second before one
of the helpers pushed the button.
And suddenly, there you were, pale
blue eyes open, eyelashes fluttering,

the throng around you able to breathe again,
you, back on the side of the living.

Bye-bye, Loss said, releasing me.
For now, Grief said, already fading.
There you go, Hope whispered,
as my life restarted with one
heartbeat:

yours.

14. The first law of thermodynamics

No energy gets created in the universe,
and none is destroyed.

So although his physical body lies stilled,
breathless, or she who still lives sits vacant,
absent without leave, a shell of her former self,

the photons that careened from their smiles,
the electricity of their touch,
their energy goes on forever—

not just in you, who carries their DNA,
the color of their eyes, their very cells
in your own—

but they exist forever in the universe
along with trillions of other particles
that yours will one day join.

It's the law of conservation of energy:
Nothing comes to be or perishes.
The energy we imagine as ours
does not belong to us; we belong to it,

transformed from one form into another.

There is no *there*, no *here*.

In the end we are all simply rearranged,
our atoms repurposed, ping-ponging
through space with all those who
ever lived—humans, leaves, amoeba—

some who breathed and walked upright,
who occupied the forms in which we loved them
for not nearly long enough.

15. Walking the fridge

(for Curtis... and my mother)

It goes back to the college boyfriend
with the vision impairment who taught
me to always cap the toothpaste,
never to leave a clear glass in the sink,
and always tuck sharp knives into
the mini butcher block on the countertop
where they were less likely to do either
of us injury.

We used to joke that the mostly blind guy
could chop vegetables better and faster
than the nearsighted girl, whose fingers
bore telltale evidence of accidental
self-stabbings. No wonder the Girl
Scout leader gently removed that girl's
whittling knife from her blood-spotted
hands—and didn't give it back for years.

But the blind boyfriend had a sixth sense
for where things lay in space—the guy who
whipped down the bike trail on two fast
wheels—possessing a kind of radar that I

don't and I so wish my mother did as
her sight dims.

He and I in those heady, early days of love
walked the fridge and cupboards after
trips to the store, making sure that he could
find things—which he did, often more easily
than I.

Now, almost a half century later, Mom
stands before her open fridge, blinded
by the light as she tries to discern honey
mustard from shapely bottles of electrolytes.
I walk the fridge with her, the two of us standing
there letting the cold out (which could get
you yelled at as a kid), as I point out three
containers of egg salad and one of tuna along
with the new salami and cheese packages
atop the cheese sticks of Colby jack.

Mom runs her hands over the just-brought-home
lunch leftovers in their traveling container,
as well as the circumference of the receptable
that shelters her special fruit—blueberries,
strawberries, bananas—that her favorite
restaurant assembles for her. She traces
outlines of small water bottles that sidle

up to Moscato chilling in thick glass.

And, when she's committed to memory
the locations of the to-be-consumed,
she edges away from the chill and says,
That's good. I've got it.

And I marvel again at the ability of these
beloveds who channel shapes into
visual memory, those who can't see
the details of my face but who swear
they'd know me anywhere.

And I believe them.

16. Onion

(for Dr. Janis Lightman)

Dr. Janis peers through the magical
machine that looks like a giant pair
of glasses on a swinging pole—
something Elton might have worn
onstage in the 1970s—
her eyes on the opposite side
of the device inspecting mine.

She's done this for years, keeping
watch on conditions that, little by little,
darken and narrow my view.
Some can be helped; some cannot.

The eye, she tells me, is as plump
and translucent as a pearl onion
when we are young, allowing light
to easily pass through the dome-
shaped cornea that helps us focus,
through the pupil and the lens,
to land on the retina that turns
light into electrical signals, zings
them through the optic nerve

to the brain, which translates
them into images.

As our eyes age, she says, the supple
layers of onion harden and yellow,
making it harder for light to reach us.

As she looks deeply into my eyes,
I think of my aging layers of onion,
wishing that I might gently peel off
the crackly covering as easily as
slicing into a fragrant bulb to make
soup, somehow returning the pearly
onions of my youth to my ocular field.

No wonder I cry when I take apart
an onion, watching its tightly bound
sections loosen and fall on the cutting
surface. Tears fall as I inhale its aroma,
as I chop it into small pieces that will
vanish when they morph into soup,
becoming something I can no longer see
no matter how hard I look.

17. You still haven't met all the people who are going to love you

It's in freeping neon, my friend,
and if that's not a literal sign,
I don't know what is.

I don't care how old you are,
how odd looking or sounding
you think you are:

Someone you don't yet know
is gonna love schlubby old you
because—and I'm not wrong about

this—you are not as schlubby as
you think you are. How do I know?
When we met, I knew I would

soon adore you, and I didn't care
that you mixed stripes with florals
or that you tripped over your feet,

or any of the things that you think

make you unlovable. Nope, there
was something endearing about

you from the get-go, and I'm not
the only one who has noticed.
Truly.

So chin up, buttercup. You still haven't
met all the people who are going
to love you. And oh, what a good,

good thing that is to tuck in your
pocket and carry with you to
touch now and again as you

walk through this world,
the only one we have, the one
with so many people, some of

whom—I promise—are just
gonna love your sweet old
extraordinary self.

18. Car wash

Forgive me, Father,
for I have committed
the (I hope) pardonable
sin of not only paying
for a car wash, but not

using my own two good
hands to wash Mother's
car, which I am using
a day a week to drive her

places, but which I am
also using every other day
to drive my older-than-you-
ever-knew-me self around.

That is not to say that I'm
incapable of washing a car
      —I'm not—
but there are days when
time is at a premium and
you're driving right by
the car wash with the funky
name and cute duck logo,

and something whispers
in your ear (maybe the car
itself?), *Wash me,* which
someone could well have
drawn in the month-old leaf
grit dusting the back window.

And so, heeding the call of
the almighty beckoning, I
pull in, pay the it-costs-how-
much-but-I-don't-care fee,
then pause at the maw
of the beast, unsure
if I've correctly lined up
the left front tire in the slot
to carry us through.

But divine intervention, well,
intervenes, and as it tugs me in,
thou art with me. And I
am in the back seat with Donna,
and we are moving through a
long-ago car wash, thrilled that
we do not have to wait outside,
but that we, too, get to ride along—

blessed by the holy water of
powerful squirters, watching
the hula skirt chamois dance
over the windshield, feel
ourselves buffed shiny by
the whirling dervishes
that brush up and over us,

washed by heavenly purple
soapsuds, then blown out
by a supersized hair dryer,
and emerge into the light,
both squeaky and clean,

ready to drive off into our
lives, so powerfully absolved,
so unbelievably blessed.

19. The way the days become a life

And how did that happen?
That enough 24-hour spans occur
that they become lived time,
a lifetime.

And that we are all not granted
as many as some, fewer than others
(and how we are missing those others).

And that there's no way to know
what the number will be,
or the date of our ending,
or how we are made
or by whom. Only that we are.

And we pause in gratitude
on the threshold of this new instant,
smiling at whoever you are,
those seen and unseen—

you who make us in silence,
moment by splendid moment,
breath by sweet breath.

11. You are here

Diego walks in the house calling
and will not stop until he finds me.
He's not seeking food, just reassurance.

Where are you? There you are.
You were gone, and I couldn't find you.

I'm here! I call,
knowing without looking that
he's paused in the doorway
as I type. I hear scratching
in the catbox, and I know
he's found another kind of
comfort, which makes me
shake my head:

You were just outside;
you could go out there.

But no, he covers, hops out
with sandy feet, comes to me,
still typing. He sits, looks up,
purrs.

Poki joins us, hops up
on the box next to me,
four penetrating eyes
relaying an insistent message
before they wander off
to curl into naps:

Here you are.
Here you truly are.

21. This longest night

So much good arrives
at precisely the worst moments,
though we can't see it for the flames,
the seizure, the accident, the illness,
for the unknown thing that has befallen us.

The way, it turns out, has been made,
has always been made for us, even as
we lose our jobs, our minds, our beloveds,

as we see the hands of people lifting
the terrified child from the boat just
traveled over rough seas, full of
haggard faces of those seeking sanctuary,

and the strangers who emerge from
the darkness bearing their particular
kind of light: the cup of water, a morsel
of food, a warm blanket, bandages,
medicine for body and soul.

What we don't see when something
is taken away is the thing being born
underneath, the new bud on the hibernating

branch. Awash in grief, in pain, in panic,
we forget.

Just wait. Take a breath. And another.
And another. You're safe. You're held.
So much good lies ahead
on the darkest day, this longest night.
Tomorrow you'll see more light.

22. Blue-sky miracle

run your fingers like a prayer
over every bit of the world,
saying quietly, with each
breath, thank you for
this chance to love

—Kai Skye

because if *thank you* is perhaps
the best prayer, then we cannot
utter it often enough

because if the world has offered
itself to us as this blue-sky miracle,
then how can we do anything but

love it, even with all its storm clouds,
its human-made devastation?
Because we are the only ones

who can love our planet and each
other enough to mend what we have
ruptured, what has been riven

like a log split with brutal force,
like fabric savagely torn. Let us be
the stitcher of seams, of echoing

prayer, the thankful breath,
the quiet love that seeps, with
great gentleness, into every

heartfelt *hello*.